Title: **Leading with Purpose: Women Transforming Nonprofits and Communities**

Char Dennis, EDD

Published by CHAR DENNIS / 1KMEG PR
ISBN 978-1-300-72536-7

Leading with Purpose: Women Transforming Nonprofits and Communities

1: The Landscape of Nonprofit Leadership

The Role of Women in Nonprofit Organizations

The role of women in nonprofit organizations has become increasingly vital in shaping the landscape of community engagement and social change. Women have historically been the backbone of the nonprofit sector, often serving as volunteers, board members, and leaders who drive missions forward. Their unique perspectives and experiences contribute to more inclusive decision-making processes, leading to more effective programs and initiatives. As the nonprofit sector continues to evolve, the influence of women in leadership positions is essential for addressing the complex challenges that communities face today.

Women in nonprofit leadership bring diverse skills and approaches to their roles. Women leaders excel in collaboration and community engagement, often characterized by strong interpersonal skills, emotional intelligence, and an ability to build consensus. These traits are fundamental in the nonprofit sector, where fostering relationships with stakeholders, donors, and community members is crucial for success. By leveraging their strengths, women leaders can create a culture of inclusivity and support that empowers their teams and the communities they serve.

Moreover, women in nonprofit organizations play a significant role in advocating for marginalized populations. Their leadership often reflects a commitment to social justice and equity, driving initiatives that address systemic issues such as poverty, education, and health disparities. Women leaders frequently prioritize the voices and needs of underrepresented people, ensuring that programs are designed with input from the communities they aim to serve. This focus on advocacy enhances the effectiveness of nonprofit initiatives and fosters a sense of ownership and empowerment among community members.

The increasing presence of women in nonprofit leadership also indicates broader societal changes regarding gender roles and expectations. As more women pursue higher education and professional development, they have the skills and knowledge necessary for nonprofit leadership positions. This shift not only benefits the organizations themselves but also inspires future generations of women aspiring to lead. By breaking through barriers and demonstrating their capabilities, women leaders in the nonprofit sector contribute to a more equitable and just society.

In conclusion, the role of women in nonprofit organizations is integral to the success of community development efforts. Their leadership styles, commitment to advocacy, and ability to foster collaboration create a foundation for transformative change. As the nonprofit sector continues to grow and adapt, empowering women to step into leadership roles will be essential for addressing the diverse needs of communities. Supporting and promoting women in nonprofit leadership enhances organizational effectiveness and paves the way for a more inclusive and equitable future.

Historical Perspectives on Women Leaders

Throughout history, women have played pivotal roles in leadership within nonprofit organizations and community development, often overcoming societal barriers and stereotypes. The historical perspectives on women leaders reveal a rich tapestry of contributions that shaped the nonprofit sector and transformed communities. From the early suffragists advocating for women's rights to contemporary leaders addressing social justice issues, women have consistently demonstrated their capacity to lead effectively and inspire change.

In the 19th and early 20th centuries, women like Jane Addams and Lillian Wald emerged as trailblazers in social reform. Addams co-founded Hull House in Chicago, providing essential services to immigrants while advocating for labor rights and public health reforms. Similarly, Wald's work with the Henry Street Settlement in New York City highlighted the importance of social work and community organization. These early leaders laid the groundwork for modern nonprofit practices, emphasizing the need for social equity and community engagement—a foundation that continues to resonate in today's nonprofit leadership.

The mid-20th century saw more women stepping into leadership roles amid the civil rights movement and the push for gender equality. Figures such as Shirley Chisholm and Betty Friedan fought for women's rights and broader social changes that affected marginalized communities. Their activism illustrated the interconnectedness of gender, race, and class issues, expanding the scope of what it meant to be a leader in the nonprofit sector. These leaders inspired a generation of women to pursue careers in public service, reinforcing the idea that effective leadership requires a commitment to social justice and community empowerment.

As the 21st century unfolded, the landscape for women leaders in nonprofits began to evolve significantly. The rise of technology and social media provided new platforms for women to amplify their voices and mobilize communities. Leaders such as Melinda Gates and Sheryl Sandberg have utilized their influence to advocate for gender equity and philanthropy, highlighting the importance of women's leadership in addressing global challenges. Their efforts underscore the necessity of leveraging resources and networks to foster sustainable change in communities, demonstrating that women leaders are crucial to advancing nonprofit missions.

In conclusion, the historical perspectives on women leaders reveal a profound legacy of resilience, innovation, and commitment to community service. Women have continuously shaped the nonprofit sector from early pioneers to contemporary advocates and contributed to significant societal changes. Recognizing and honoring this history empowers current and future women leaders, and the band enriches the broader narrative of leadership in public relations and educational leadership. As we move forward, it is essential to build on this legacy, ensuring that women's voices remain central to the ongoing efforts to create equitable and thriving communities.

Current Trends and Statistics

The landscape of nonprofit leadership is evolving, with an increasing number of women stepping into significant roles within organizational roles, revealing that women now hold approximately 50% of nonprofit executive positions, a notable increase from previous decades. This shift indicates a growing recognition of the valuable perspectives and leadership styles women bring to the sector. Furthermore, women-led nonprofits are often more focused on movement and social impact, emphasizing collaboration, inclusivity, and sustainability in their initiatives.

Research highlights that organizations led by women tend to prioritize the needs of marginalized communities, often resulting in more effective programs and services. Women leaders are frequently driven by personal experiences and a commitment to social justice, which catalyzes their efforts to address systemic issues. Statistical analyses show that nonprofits with female executives are more likely to implement practices that enhance community involvement and advocacy, demonstrating a connection between gender diversity in leadership and organizational effectiveness.

The importance of mentorship and support networks for women in nonprofit leadership is increasingly recognized. Current trends indicate that women are more likely to succeed in executive roles when they benefit from formal mentorship programs and peer networks. These resources help women navigate challenges within the nonprofit sector and foster a culture of collaboration and shared learning. As women leaders continue to advocate for their peers, they create pathways for future generations, ensuring that the impact of their leadership extends beyond their immediate roles.

Data also underscores the economic impact of women's leadership in nonprofits. Studies show that organizations with female leadership experience higher funding and donor engagement rates. This is attributed to the unique ability of women leaders to cultivate relationships and tell compelling stories that resonate with diverse audiences. Women-led nonprofits often attract a broader base of volunteers and stakeholders, enhancing their overall reach and effectiveness in community service.

As we continue to explore the current trends and statistics surrounding women in nonprofit leadership, it is evident that their contributions are reshaping the sector. The increasing presence of women in leadership positions reflects changing societal norms and drives innovation and responsiveness within the nonprofit landscape. Organizations can better serve their communities and create lasting change by fostering inclusive environments that celebrate diverse leadership. This evolution in leadership dynamics underscores women's critical role in transforming nonprofits and enhancing community development efforts.

2: Defining Purpose in Leadership

Understanding Personal and Organizational Purpose

Understanding personal and organizational purpose is fundamental to effective leadership, particularly in the nonprofit sector. For women in leadership roles, clarity for personal and organizational purposes serves as a guiding beacon that informs decision-making, inspires teams, and engages communities. Personal purpose reflects an individual's core values, passions, and motivations, while organizational purpose articulates a nonprofit's mission, vision, and goals. Together, these elements create a cohesive narrative that aligns individual actions with the organization's broader objectives, fostering a shared commitment to community empowerment and social change.

In nonprofit organizations, a well-defined purpose is crucial for establishing credibility and trust among stakeholders. It not only helps attract funding and resources but also motivates staff and volunteers by giving them a sense of belonging and direction. Nonprofits led by women often embody a unique perspective on purpose, emphasizing collaboration, inclusiveness, and community engagement. By articulating a clear organizational purpose, women leaders can engage diverse groups, ensuring their initiatives resonate with the values and needs of their communities.

Personal purpose is equally significant for women in nonprofit leadership. It drives passion, resilience, and the ability to navigate challenges inherent in the sector. When women leaders know their purpose, they can better communicate their vision and inspire others to join their cause. This alignment between personal and organizational purpose helps create a culture of authenticity, where leaders are seen as figureheads and genuine advocates for their mission. This authenticity is particularly compelling in public relations and higher education, where trust and credibility are paramount.

Moreover, understanding and articulating purpose allows women leaders to be more strategic in their approaches to community development. By identifying the specific needs of their communities, they can tailor their programs and initiatives to address those needs effectively. This strategic alignment with personal and organizational purpose ensures that resources are utilized efficiently, maximizing impact. Women leaders can leverage their unique experiences and insights to create transformative programs that reflect their values while addressing systemic community issues.

In conclusion, the interplay between personal and organizational purpose is vital for women in nonprofit leadership. By fostering a deep understanding of their motivations alongside the mission of their organizations, these leaders can create powerful narratives that drive change. Emphasizing purpose enhances leadership effectiveness and empowers communities to engage actively in the change process. As women continue to lead in the nonprofit sector, their commitment to purpose will be instrumental in shaping a more equitable and just society.

Aligning Values with Mission

Aligning values with mission is a crucial aspect of effective leadership in the nonprofit sector, particularly for women leading organizations aimed at empowering communities and fostering change. In the context of public relations and higher education, this alignment ensures that the organization communicates its objectives clearly and resonates with stakeholders on a deeper level. When leaders articulate their core values, they set a foundation for their mission, guiding decision-making processes and enhancing trust among constituents.

For women in nonprofit leadership, embodying an organization's values can significantly impact its community engagement efforts. A mission that reflects shared values fosters a sense of ownership among staff and volunteers, encouraging them to invest emotionally in the organization's goals. This collaborative spirit is essential for building strong relationships with community members, as it demonstrates a commitment to shared ideals and a willingness to work together towards common objectives. Leaders can cultivate an environment where diverse perspectives contribute to a more inclusive mission by actively engaging stakeholders in discussions about values.

Aligning values with mission is vital in strategic planning and resource allocation. Women leaders must ensure that their organizations are mission-driven and value-driven, as this alignment informs the selection of programs and initiatives that will be pursued. By prioritizing projects that reflect the organization's core values, leaders can maximize their impact and enhance their credibility within the community. This alignment is a guiding principle for measuring success and evaluating outcomes, ensuring that every effort contributes to the overarching mission.

Moreover, aligning values with mission is essential in maintaining organizational integrity and transparency. In an era where stakeholders demand accountability and ethical practices, women leaders must be vigilant in upholding their stated values in every aspect of their organization's operations. This consistency strengthens the organization's reputation and fosters a culture of trust where employees and community members feel confident in their leadership. By openly communicating how values inform daily practices and decision-making, leaders can reinforce their commitment to their mission and cultivate a loyal supporter base.

In conclusion, aligning values with mission is a fundamental principle for women in nonprofit leadership, particularly in public relations and higher education. This alignment enhances community engagement and trust, guides strategic planning, and ensures organizational integrity. By actively promoting and embodying shared values, women leaders can empower their communities, create meaningful change, and inspire others to join them in their mission. The journey towards alignment is ongoing, requiring regular reflection and adaptation to ensure that values and mission remain relevant and impactful in the ever-evolving landscape of nonprofit leadership.

The Impact of Purpose-Driven Leadership

Purpose-driven leadership is a transformative approach that significantly shapes the landscape of nonprofits and community development. This leadership style emphasizes a clear vision and mission that resonates with organizational goals and community needs. For women in nonprofit leadership, adopting a purpose-driven framework allows for aligning personal values with professional objectives, fostering an environment where passion meets strategic action. This alignment is particularly crucial in educational settings, where leaders are tasked with shaping the organizational culture and the broader community impact.

One of the most notable impacts of purpose-driven leadership is creating a strong organizational culture that encourages collaboration and innovation. Women leaders often bring unique perspectives and experiences to their roles, which can inspire diverse teams to work toward a common goal. This inclusivity fosters a sense of belonging and empowerment among staff and stakeholders, increasing engagement and productivity. In educational institutions, where collaboration is essential for success, purpose-driven leadership can break down silos and promote interdisciplinary approaches that enrich the learning experience.

Moreover, purpose-driven leaders are adept at building relationships with various stakeholders, including donors, community members, and governmental agencies. These leaders can cultivate trust and support by clearly articulating their mission and demonstrating a genuine commitment to their purpose. This trust is essential for securing funding and resources, which are often vital for the sustainability of nonprofit organizations. In higher education, where community partnerships are increasingly important, women leaders who embody purpose-driven principles can effectively engage with diverse groups to foster collaborative initiatives that enhance educational opportunities.

The impact of purpose-driven leadership extends beyond organizational success; it also contributes to social change and empowerment within the community. Women leaders who prioritizing purpose are more likely to advocate for marginalized voices and address systemic inequalities. This advocacy is critical in nonprofit work, where the aim is often to uplift communities and create lasting change. By integrating their purpose into community development efforts, these leaders enhance their organizations' effectiveness and inspire others to join in the mission of social justice and equity.

Finally, the legacy of purpose-driven leadership is profound, particularly for women in nonprofit roles. As they model purposefulness in their leadership styles, they pave the way for future generations of leaders. This legacy is crucial in educational environments, where students and aspiring leaders can learn from the examples set by women who have successfully navigated challenges while remaining committed to their mission. By fostering a culture of purpose-driven leadership, women can ensure that the values of empowerment, equity, and community engagement continue to thrive in nonprofit and educational sectors, ultimately leading to a more just and inclusive society.

3: Building Community Through Collaboration

The Importance of Partnerships

Partnerships play a crucial role in amplifying the impact of nonprofit organizations, especially those led by women who are transforming communities. By fostering collaboration between various stakeholders, including other nonprofits, government entities, and private sector organizations, women leaders can leverage resources, knowledge, and networks to address complex social issues. These partnerships enable organizations to reach broader audiences, enhance their credibility, and increase their capacity to effect change. In the nonprofit sector, where resources are often limited, strategic alliances can provide essential support and sustainability for initiatives to empower communities.

Establishing effective partnerships requires clear communication and shared goals among all parties involved. Women in leadership positions often bring unique perspectives and collaborative skills that can facilitate these discussions. By actively engaging with partners and involving them in decision-making, women leaders can create a sense of ownership and commitment to the shared mission. This collaborative approach strengthens relationships and fosters innovation, as diverse viewpoints can lead to more creative solutions for community challenges.

Additionally, partnerships can enhance the visibility of initiatives and increase access to funding opportunities. Funders are more likely to invest in projects demonstrating collaboration among multiple organizations, which indicates a broader support base and a higher likelihood of success. Women leaders in nonprofits can utilize their networks to forge connections that may lead to financial backing and resources necessary for program development. By showcasing the collective impact of their work, these leaders can effectively advocate for their initiatives and attract more support.

Moreover, partnerships can facilitate knowledge-sharing and capacity-building among organizations. Women in nonprofit leadership often prioritize mentorship and support for emerging leaders, creating environments where skills and best practices are exchanged. Collaborative training sessions, workshops, and shared resources can empower staff and volunteers across organizations, enhancing their effectiveness and enabling them to serve their communities better. This culture of learning not only strengthens individual organizations but also contributes to the overall resilience of the nonprofit sector.

Finally, the importance of partnerships extends beyond immediate organizational goals to influence systemic change. Women-led nonprofits can challenge existing power dynamics by working together and advocating for policies that benefit marginalized communities. These collective efforts can significantly advance social justice, health equity, and education reform. Women leaders who prioritize partnerships are enhancing their organizations and paving the way for a more inclusive and equitable society. Through collaboration, they are harnessing the collective strength of their communities to create lasting change.

Engaging Stakeholders Effectively

Engaging stakeholders effectively is crucial to successful nonprofit leadership, especially for women transforming communities. Stakeholders, which include community members, donors, volunteers, and organizational partners, play a significant role in shaping the mission and impact of nonprofit organizations. Understanding these groups' diverse perspectives and needs is essential for fostering meaningful relationships that drive collaborative initiatives. Women leaders in the nonprofit sector must prioritize stakeholder engagement as a strategic approach to enhance community involvement and support for their causes.

One effective method for engaging stakeholders is through active listening. By creating spaces for open dialogue, nonprofit leaders can gain valuable insights into the concerns and aspirations of their stakeholders. This practice helps build trust and empowers stakeholders to feel valued and heard. Women leaders can leverage their unique communication styles to facilitate these discussions, ensuring that all voices are included in the decision-making process. Such inclusive practices can lead to more innovative solutions and a stronger sense of community ownership over initiatives.

Another important aspect of stakeholder engagement is transparency. Nonprofit organizations that openly share their goals, challenges, and successes foster a culture of accountability and trust. Women leaders should emphasize the importance of clear communication regarding organizational strategies and the impact of stakeholder contributions. By providing regular updates and being honest about setbacks, leaders can cultivate a loyal base of support that is informed and engaged. This transparency can also encourage more stakeholders to become active participants through volunteering, donating, or advocating for the nonprofit's mission.

Moreover, leveraging technology can significantly enhance stakeholder engagement efforts. Social media platforms, email newsletters, and virtual meetings offer innovative ways to connect with stakeholders, especially in an increasingly digital world. Women leaders should harness these tools to share stories, showcase impact, and facilitate ongoing conversations with their communities. By embracing technology, leaders can reach a broader audience, including younger generations who are often more engaged in digital spaces. This expanded reach can lead to enhanced partnerships and collaborative opportunities that benefit the organization and its stakeholders.

Lastly, it is essential to recognize and celebrate the contributions of stakeholders. Acknowledging their efforts fosters a sense of belonging and reinforces the importance of their organizational roles. Women leaders can create recognition programs or host appreciation events highlighting the achievements of volunteers, donors, and community members. By celebrating these contributions, leaders motivate stakeholders to continue their involvement and create a positive organizational culture that encourages ongoing engagement. Effective stakeholder engagement is not just about communication; it is about building lasting relationships that empower communities and drive meaningful change.

Case Studies of Successful Collaborations

In nonprofit leadership, collaborative efforts among women have proven to be a powerful catalyst for community transformation. Case studies of successful collaborations illuminate how these partnerships enhance organizational effectiveness and amplify the impact on the communities they serve. We can identify key strategies and principles that contribute to their success by examining specific instances where women-led initiatives have thrived. These case studies serve as a blueprint for others aiming to foster collaboration and drive meaningful change within their organizations.

One notable example is the partnership between a women-led nonprofit focused on education and a local university. This collaboration aimed to improve access to educational resources for underserved communities. By combining the nonprofit's grassroots knowledge and the university's academic expertise, they developed a series of workshops catering to the community's unique needs. Through shared resources and joint marketing efforts, they were able to reach a larger audience, significantly increasing participation rates in educational programs. This case highlights the importance of aligning organizational missions and leveraging each partner's strengths to achieve common goals.

Another successful collaboration was formed between a women's health organization and a local government agency. This partnership sought to address health disparities faced by women in low-income neighborhoods. By pooling their resources and expertise, the organizations launched a comprehensive health initiative that included outreach, education, and access to healthcare services. The collaboration improved health outcomes and empowered women to take charge of their health. This case underscores the value of building coalitions that unite different sectors, demonstrating how shared objectives can lead to remarkable community outcomes.

A third example can be found in a collaborative effort between women entrepreneurs and a nonprofit dedicated to economic development. This initiative focused on creating a mentorship program that connected aspiring women business owners with established leaders in the field. The program provided valuable networking opportunities, skill development, and access to funding resources. The collaboration empowered women to pursue their entrepreneurial ambitions by facilitating these connections while strengthening the local economy. This case illustrates how strategic partnerships can enhance community capacity building, particularly for marginalized groups.

Lastly, a partnership between a nonprofit advocating for environmental justice and a community college exemplifies the interaction that can result from collaboration. Together, they launched a project to educate residents about sustainable practices and environmental conservation. The community college provided academic resources and expertise, while the nonprofit engaged residents through outreach and advocacy. This collaboration raised awareness about environmental issues and fostered a sense of community ownership over local resources. The success of this initiative highlights the importance of inclusivity and community engagement in driving sustainable change, showcasing how women in nonprofit leadership can take charge of addressing pressing societal challenges.

Chapter 4: Navigating Challenges in Nonprofit Leadership

Gender Bias and Stereotypes

Gender bias and stereotypes play a significant role in shaping the experiences and opportunities available to women in nonprofit leadership. Despite the increasing number of women pursuing leadership roles, systemic biases persist, influencing organizational perceptions and decisions. These biases manifest in various ways, including assumptions about women's capabilities, leadership styles, and commitment to their roles. Understanding how these stereotypes operate is crucial for fostering an equitable environment where women can thrive as leaders and effect meaningful change in their communities.

One of the primary stereotypes affecting women in leadership is the belief that they are less competent than their male counterparts. This perception can lead to women being overlooked for promotions or leadership positions, regardless of their qualifications or accomplishments. Research has shown that women often must prove themselves more than men to gain the same recognition and authority. This biased evaluation of women's capabilities limits their career advancement and deprives organizations of the diverse perspectives and skills that women bring to leadership roles.

Furthermore, gender stereotypes often dictate the preferred leadership styles within organizations. Traditional notions of leadership frequently align with masculine characteristics, such as decisiveness and assertiveness. In contrast, traits usually associated with women, such as collaboration and empathy, are undervalued. This dichotomy creates an environment where women may feel pressured to adopt a more masculine leadership style to be taken seriously, often at the expense of their authentic selves. Such expectations can lead to a lack of confidence and increased stress, ultimately hindering their effectiveness as leaders.

The impact of gender bias extends beyond individual experiences; it can influence organizational culture and community engagement. Nonprofits led by women often adopt more inclusive practices, prioritize community needs, and foster collaborative environments. However, when gender biases persist, these organizations may struggle to realize their full potential. Addressing stereotypes and prejudice in leadership benefits women and enhances nonprofit organizations' overall effectiveness and reach, ultimately leading to a more significant community impact.

To combat gender bias and stereotypes, organizations must actively implement policies and practices to promote equality and inclusivity. This includes providing leadership training tailored to women, fostering mentorship opportunities, and creating transparent evaluation processes that mitigate biases. Additionally, organizations should encourage a culture of feedback and open dialogue, allowing for the exploration of implicit biases that may affect decision-making. By challenging stereotypes and actively supporting women in leadership, nonprofits can pave the way for transformative change within their communities, ensuring that diverse voices are heard and valued.

Funding Constraints and Resource Allocation

Funding constraints present a significant challenge for nonprofit organizations, particularly those led by women committed to empowering communities and driving change. Many nonprofits operate on limited budgets, relying heavily on donations, grants, and fundraising efforts. These financial limitations can hinder the ability of women leaders to implement their vision fully, as they must navigate the complexities of resource allocation while striving to meet the needs of their communities. By understanding these constraints, women leaders can better strategize their funding and resource management approaches, ensuring that their initiatives can thrive despite financial challenges.

Effective resource allocation is crucial in addressing the funding constraints faced by nonprofits. Women leaders must prioritize their programs and initiatives based on the immediate needs of their communities, assessing which projects will yield the most significant impact. This requires a deep understanding of the community's needs and the organization's specific strengths. Leaders should employ data-driven decision-making to evaluate the effectiveness of their programs, allowing them to allocate resources where they will be the most beneficial. Moreover, fostering a collaborative environment within the organization can encourage innovative solutions to stretch limited resources further.

In addition to strategic allocation, diversifying funding sources is essential for overcoming financial challenges. Women leaders can explore various funding avenues, including corporate sponsorships, government grants, and crowdfunding campaigns. By broadening their funding base, nonprofits can reduce dependency on a single source of income, thus enhancing financial stability. Women in leadership positions should leverage their networks and build relationships with potential funders who align with their mission, showcasing the value and impact of their work. This approach helps secure necessary funds and fosters community engagement and support.

Moreover, addressing funding constraints involves advocating for more equitable funding practices within the nonprofit sector. Women leaders should engage in conversations about systemic barriers that affect funding allocations, particularly for organizations led by women or serving marginalized populations. By raising awareness of these disparities, women can influence funding bodies to prioritize equity in their distribution processes. This advocacy benefits their organizations and paves the way for future leaders, contributing to a more just and supportive nonprofit landscape.

Lastly, resilience and adaptability are key traits for women leaders in navigating funding constraints. The ability to pivot and adjust strategies in response to changing financial landscapes is crucial for sustained success. By fostering a culture of innovation and openness to change within their organizations, women leaders can empower their teams to think creatively about overcoming obstacles. Sharing success stories and lessons learned from previous challenges can inspire confidence and collaboration, ultimately leading to a more robust and impactful nonprofit sector. Emphasizing resilience ensures that women-led nonprofits can continue to serve their communities effectively, even in the face of financial adversity.

Balancing Passion with Pragmatism

Balancing passion with pragmatism is crucial for women in nonprofit leadership roles, particularly in public relations and higher education. Passion drives the vision and commitment necessary for transformative change, but without pragmatic approaches, that vision can falter. Leaders in these sectors often find themselves at the intersection of heartfelt intentions and the practicalities of resource allocation, stakeholder expectations, and measurable outcomes. Embracing both elements allows women to champion causes effectively while ensuring the sustainability of their initiatives.

In the nonprofit landscape, passion can inspire and mobilize communities. It is the driving force behind campaigns that address social injustices, enhance educational opportunities, and advocate for underrepresented voices. However, this enthusiasm must be matched with a strategic mindset. Leaders must evaluate the needs of their communities, analyze data to inform decisions and create actionable plans that lead to tangible results. This pragmatic approach does not dilute passion but channels it into structured frameworks that facilitate success and accountability.

Furthermore, balancing passion and pragmatism requires adept communication skills, especially in public relations. Leaders must articulate their vision compellingly while also addressing the practical concerns of stakeholders. This involves crafting emotionally resonating narratives while providing clear, factual evidence of the initiative's potential impact. Effective communication fosters trust and buy-in from community members and funding partners, which is essential for the longevity of any nonprofit endeavor. Women leaders can leverage their unique perspectives and experiences to bridge the gap between aspiration and execution.

Additionally, cultivating a culture of collaboration is vital to harmonizing passion with pragmatism. In educational leadership and community development, partnerships can amplify efforts and resources. Women can share insights, strategies, and support systems that enhance their initiatives by engaging with other organizations, educators, and community leaders. Collaborative approaches encourage diverse viewpoints, enriching the decision-making process and leading to more well-rounded solutions addressing complex community challenges.

Ultimately, the ability to balance passion with pragmatism is not only beneficial for individual leaders but also for the communities they serve. A strategic focus ensures that passionate initiatives are rooted in reality, allowing for sustained impact. Women in nonprofit leadership must embrace this duality, recognizing that their heartfelt commitment to change is most powerful when paired with practical strategies. This synergy drives success and inspires future generations of leaders to approach their work with both fervor and a clear-eyed understanding of the challenges they face.

Chapter 5: Leadership Styles and Their Impact

Transformational Leadership

Transformational leadership is a pivotal concept in the realm of nonprofit organizations, particularly as it pertains to women leading these initiatives. This leadership style emphasizes motivation, inspiration, and fostering an environment where followers can achieve their full potential. Women in nonprofit leadership often embody transformational leadership qualities, championing causes that resonate deeply with their communities. This approach enhances organizational effectiveness and empowers individuals to take ownership of their roles in fostering community development and social change.

One of the defining characteristics of transformational leadership is the ability to inspire a shared vision. Women leaders in nonprofit organizations frequently leverage their experiences and insights to articulate a compelling narrative that aligns with the values and aspirations of their communities. By engaging stakeholders and fostering collaboration, these leaders create a sense of shared purpose that transcends individual interests. This collective vision catalyzes mobilizing resources, nurturing innovation, and driving meaningful change within the community.

In addition to vision, transformational leaders prioritize their team members' personal and professional development. This focus on individual growth is particularly significant in the nonprofit sector, where resources can be limited, and the workforce often consists of volunteers or individuals driven by passion rather than financial incentives. Women leaders foster mentorship and provide opportunities for skill development, encouraging their teams to take initiative and embrace leadership roles. This enhances the organization's capacity and cultivates a culture of empowerment and inclusivity.

Moreover, transformational leadership is considered by a strong ethical foundation and a commitment to social justice. Women leaders often bring a unique perspective to their organizations, emphasizing the importance of equity, diversity, and community engagement. Their approach involves actively listening to the voices of marginalized groups and ensuring that their needs are represented in decision-making processes. This commitment to inclusivity strengthens the organization's legitimacy, builds trust, and fosters a sense of belonging within the community.

Finally, the impact of transformational leadership extends beyond the immediate organization to the broader community. By championing social change and advocating for sustainable development, nonprofit women leaders play a crucial role in addressing systemic issues affecting their communities. Their ability to mobilize support and galvanize action around pressing social issues positions them as key change agents. As they continue to inspire and empower others, these leaders contribute to a legacy of transformational leadership that has the potential to reshape communities and create lasting impact.

Servant Leadership and Community Focus

Servant leadership is a philosophy that prioritizes the community's needs and empowers individuals to contribute positively to society. In nonprofit organizations, this leadership style fosters an environment where collaboration and mutual respect thrive. Women in nonprofit leadership often embody these principles, leveraging their unique experiences and perspectives to create inclusive spaces that encouraging community engagement. By adopting a servant leadership approach, women leaders can effectively mobilize resources and inspire collective action, ultimately enhancing the impact of their organizations on the communities they serve.

At the heart of servant leadership is the commitment to serving others. This perspective shifts the focus from a traditional top-down leadership model to one where leaders prioritize the growth and well-being of their team members and the communities they affect. Women leaders often bring a relational focus to their work, understanding that strong relationships are crucial for achieving long-term goals. By nurturing these connections, they can cultivate trust within their organizations and the broader community, facilitating collaboration and shared purpose among diverse stakeholders.

Community focus is integral to the success of nonprofit organizations, especially in educational leadership. Women leaders who embrace servant leadership principles are well-positioned to identify the unique needs of their communities and respond with relevant programs and initiatives. This community-centric approach enhances the effectiveness of nonprofit efforts and empowers individuals within the community to take ownership of their development. By involving community members in decision-making processes, women leaders create a sense of belonging and accountability, reinforcing that everyone has a role in fostering positive change.

Moreover, servant leadership encourages continuous learning and adaptation, essential in the ever-evolving landscape of nonprofit work. Women leaders who model this adaptability inspire their teams to remain agile in facing challenges. By prioritizing feedback and fostering a culture of open communication, leaders can ensure that their organizations remain responsive to the needs of their communities. This iterative process of learning and adjustment strengthens the organization and builds resilience within the community, equipping individuals to navigate future challenges effectively.

The impact of servant leadership and community focus extends beyond individual organizations; it can potentially transform entire communities. As women leaders exemplify these values, they inspire others to adopt similar approaches, creating a ripple effect of positive change. This transformation is particularly significant in educational leadership, where the partnership between nonprofits and academic institutions can lead to innovative solutions for pressing social issues. By continually fostering a culture of service and community engagement, women leaders elevate their organizations and contribute to the broader goal of social equity and empowerment for all.

Adaptive Leadership in Times of Change

Adaptive leadership is essential in navigating the complexities of change, particularly within the nonprofit sector and educational institutions. This leadership style emphasizes flexibility, resilience, and the capacity to respond to the dynamic needs of communities. Women leaders in nonprofit organizations often face unique challenges, including limited resources, shifting priorities, and diverse stakeholder expectations. By embracing adaptive leadership, these women can effectively guide their organizations through periods of uncertainty, ensuring they remain aligned with their mission while fostering community engagement and development.

At the core of adaptive leadership is assessing the environment and identifying the challenges that require a response. Women leaders must be keenly aware of social, economic, and political factors influencing their organizations and the communities they serve. This involves gathering data, engaging in stakeholder dialogue, and remaining open to new ideas and perspectives. By creating an inclusive atmosphere where voices are heard, women leaders can better understand the needs of their communities and develop strategies that resonate with those they aim to serve.

In times of change, adaptive leaders must also prioritize collaboration and innovation. Women in nonprofit leadership roles can leverage their networks and partnerships to foster collective problem-solving and resource-sharing. Encouraging cooperation between team members and community stakeholders enhances creativity, builds trust, and strengthens relationships. This collaborative spirit is particularly vital in addressing the evolving challenges faced by nonprofits and educational institutions, as it allows for diverse ideas to emerge and fosters a sense of shared ownership in the solutions developed.

Another critical aspect of adaptive leadership is navigating resistance and uncertainty. Change often brings discomfort, and leaders must be prepared to address concerns and fears among their teams and communities. Women leaders can utilize their empathetic approach to address these emotions, fostering a culture of resilience and adaptability. By sharing their experiences with change, they can inspire others to embrace transformation as a pathway to growth and development, ultimately reinforcing the organization's commitment to its mission.

Finally, adaptive leadership in times of change requires ongoing learning and reflection. Women leaders should model a growth mindset, recognizing that failure is an opportunity for learning and improvement. By encouraging continuous professional development and supporting team members in their personal growth journeys, these leaders can create a culture that values innovation and adaptability. In doing so, they empower their organizations to thrive in changing environments and position themselves as role models for future generations of women leaders in the nonprofit and educational sectors.

Chapter 6: Empowering Others: Mentorship and Development

The Importance of Mentoring in Nonprofits

Mentoring is crucial in the nonprofit sector, particularly for women in leadership positions. Within this context, mentoring is a vital tool for professional development, fostering skills, and building networks essential for effective leadership. Women often face unique challenges in navigating their careers, including gender biases and limited access to influential networks. By establishing strong mentoring relationships, women leaders can gain valuable insights, encouragement, and support that propel them toward success. This focus on mentorship benefits individual leaders and strengthens nonprofit organizations' overall capacity to fulfill their missions.

The significance of mentoring in nonprofits extends beyond personal growth; it is instrumental in cultivating a culture of collaboration and support. When women leaders mentor others, they create a ripple effect that empowers the next generation of women in the sector. This mentorship cycle fosters an environment where knowledge and experiences are shared, leading to enhanced organizational performance and more significant community impact. Nonprofits prioritizing mentorship can develop a more inclusive and equitable workplace, ultimately benefiting their communities. By championing the importance of mentoring, organizations can address systemic barriers and promote diversity within their leadership ranks.

Mentoring relationships can take various forms, including formal programs, informal connections, and peer mentoring. Each type offers distinct advantages that cater to different needs and preferences. Formal mentoring programs, often structured by organizations, provide a clear framework for pairing mentors and mentees, setting goals, and measuring outcomes. On the other hand, informal connections allow for more organic relationships to form, enabling women to seek guidance from peers or established leaders based on shared experiences and interests. Peer mentoring creates a supportive environment where women can exchange ideas, challenges, and strategies, reinforcing that collaboration is key to success in the nonprofit sector.

Moreover, the impact of mentorship is amplified when organizations invest in training and resources for mentors and mentees. Equipping mentors with the necessary skills to guide and support their mentees effectively enhances the quality of the mentoring relationship. Workshops, seminars, and networking events can provide mentors with tools to navigate challenging conversations and foster growth in their mentees. Likewise, providing mentees with access to professional development opportunities ensures they are prepared to take full advantage of the guidance they receive. This investment in mentorship strengthens individual capabilities and contributes to the overall effectiveness of nonprofit organizations.

In conclusion, the importance of mentoring in nonprofits cannot be overstated. It is a powerful mechanism for personal and professional growth, promoting collaboration, and addressing systemic inequalities within the sector. For women in nonprofit leadership, mentoring provides a pathway to success, enabling them to overcome challenges and create meaningful change in their communities. By prioritizing mentorship and fostering a culture of support, nonprofit organizations can empower women leaders, enhance their organizational effectiveness, and ultimately drive more significant impact in their communities.

Developing Future Women Leaders

Developing future women leaders is crucial to building resilient nonprofits and fostering community engagement. Women have historically faced barriers in leadership roles, particularly within the nonprofit sector, where representation has lagged behind that of their male counterparts. Organizations must implement targeted initiatives to address this disparity that nurture and empower emerging female leaders. By investing in mentorship programs, providing professional development opportunities, and encouraging women to take on leadership roles, nonprofits can create a pipeline of capable leaders prepared to navigate the complexities of community needs.

Mentorship plays a pivotal role in the development of future women leaders. Establishing formal mentorship programs within nonprofits can facilitate knowledge transfer and offer emerging leaders the guidance they need to succeed. Experienced professionals can share their insights on navigating organizational challenges, building networks, and developing strategic thinking skills. This relationship fosters confidence and helps women envision themselves in leadership positions. Moreover, mentorship can provide access to resources and opportunities that women may not otherwise encounter, ensuring they are equipped to lead effectively.

Professional development opportunities tailored to women are essential for enhancing skills and competencies. Workshops, training sessions, and conferences on leadership development can empower women to hone their communication, negotiation, and conflict-resolution abilities. By prioritizing these educational experiences, organizations signal their commitment to cultivating female talent. Additionally, partnering with academic institutions to create specialized programs can further enhance the skill sets of women in the nonprofit sector, providing them with the tools necessary to enact meaningful change within their communities.

Encouraging women to take on nonprofit leadership roles is critical for creating a diverse and inclusive organizational culture. Organizations should actively promote policies that support women's advancement, such as flexible work arrangements and equitable pay practices. By fostering an environment where women feel valued and supported, nonprofits can increase retention rates and build a more diverse leadership team. Furthermore, highlighting successful women leaders within the organization can inspire others, reinforcing that women can and should occupy leadership positions.

Developing future women leaders requires a multifaceted approach that addresses systemic barriers and fosters an inclusive culture. By prioritizing mentorship, professional development, and supportive policies, nonprofits can empower women to rise to leadership roles and drive transformative change in their communities. As women take their place at the forefront of nonprofit leadership, they will shape the sector's future and inspire the next generation of leaders to continue the journey toward equality and empowerment.

Creating a Culture of Empowerment

Creating a culture of empowerment within nonprofit organizations is essential for fostering sustainable change and enhancing community engagement. Empowerment involves enabling individuals, particularly women in leadership roles, to take ownership of their work and decisions, creating an environment where their contributions are valued. In the context of public relations and higher education, it is crucial to develop strategies that promote individual growth and align with the organization's overarching mission. By embracing a culture of empowerment, nonprofits can inspire their teams to innovate, collaborate, and effectively address the communities' needs.

One fundamental aspect of fostering a culture of empowerment is the establishment of clear communication channels. Open and transparent communication ensures that all organization members feel heard and valued. This is particularly important in educational leadership, where diverse perspectives contribute to the richness of decision-making. Leaders should encourage feedback and actively solicit input from team members at all levels. By creating forums for discussion, whether through regular meetings or digital platforms, organizations can cultivate an environment of trust where individuals feel safe to express their ideas and concerns.

Training and professional development play a significant role in empowering women leaders within nonprofits. Providing access to resources that enhance skills and knowledge boosts confidence and equips individuals to tackle complex challenges effectively. Organizations should prioritize mentorship programs and workshops on leadership development, strategic planning, and community engagement. These initiatives not only uplift women but also create a pipeline of skilled leaders who can drive the mission of the nonprofit forward, ensuring that the organization remains responsive to community needs.

Recognition and celebrating achievements are also vital in creating a culture of empowerment. Acknowledging the contributions of team members fosters a sense of belonging and motivates individuals to strive for excellence. This can be achieved through formal recognition programs and informal celebrations of milestones and successes. By publicly acknowledging women's hard work and dedication in leadership roles, organizations reinforce the value of their contributions, encouraging others to pursue leadership opportunities and take initiative within their communities.

Finally, fostering a culture of empowerment requires a commitment to inclusivity and diversity. Organizations must actively seek to create a diverse leadership team that reflects their communities. This not only enhances decision-making but also ensures that a variety of voices are represented in the organization's initiatives. By prioritizing diversity, nonprofits can harness the strengths and perspectives of all individuals, ultimately leading to more innovative solutions to community challenges. In doing so, they empower women in leadership and build a more equitable and responsive nonprofit sector poised to create meaningful change.

Chapter 7: Strategic Communication in Nonprofit Leadership

Crafting Your Organization's Narrative

Crafting your organization's narrative is essential for women leaders in the nonprofit sector, particularly within educational leadership and community development. A compelling narrative communicates your mission and vision and establishes an emotional connection with your audience. This connection is vital for garnering support, attracting donors, and inspiring volunteers. By weaving together your organization's core values and stories, you create a framework that resonates with stakeholders and highlights the unique contributions of women in leadership roles.

The first step in crafting your organization's narrative is identifying the key themes that define your mission. Focus on the issues your organization addresses and the communities you serve. Understand the challenges these communities face and the impact your organization aims to achieve. This clarity will allow you to articulate an authentic and relatable narrative. Engage with team members, beneficiaries, and community partners to gather perspectives and anecdotes to enrich your narrative, ensuring it reflects the voices of those you serve.

Once you have established the foundational themes, it is essential to incorporate personal stories that exemplify the work. Stories humanize your mission and illustrate the real-life implications of your organization's efforts. Highlight the experiences of women leaders within your organization and their journeys towards empowerment and community impact. These narratives can serve as powerful testimonials that showcase individual achievements and demonstrate women's collective strength in nonprofit leadership.

Your narrative should also address the broader context of nonprofit work and the importance of community involvement. In an increasingly complex era of social issues, it is imperative to articulate how your organization fits into the larger landscape of community development and educational leadership. Position your organization as a catalyst for change, emphasizing collaboration and partnership as central themes. This approach strengthens your narrative and invites others to engage in your mission, fostering a sense of shared purpose.

Finally, remember that crafting your organization's narrative is an ongoing process. As your organization evolves, so too should your narrative. Regularly revisit and revise your story to reflect new achievements, challenges, and shifts in the community landscape. Encourage feedback from stakeholders to ensure your narrative remains relevant and impactful. By maintaining an adaptive narrative, you solidify your organization's presence in the community and continue inspiring action and engagement among women leaders and supporters.

Utilizing Social Media and Digital Platforms

Social media and digital platforms have become essential tools for women in nonprofit leadership, enabling them to amplify their voices, engage with their communities, and drive impactful change. By leveraging these platforms, leaders can effectively share their missions, connect with supporters, and mobilize resources. In an era where online presence often translates to influence, understanding how to utilize these tools is crucial for promoting causes and fostering community development.

One of the primary advantages of social media is its ability to reach diverse audiences quickly and effectively. Women leaders can utilize platforms like Facebook, Twitter, Instagram, and LinkedIn to disseminate information about their organizations and initiatives. By creating compelling content and engaging narratives, they can capture the attention of potential supporters, volunteers, and donors. Furthermore, these platforms allow for real-time interaction, enabling leaders to promptly respond to inquiries and feedback, thereby building trust and fostering a sense of community among followers.

Digital storytelling is another critical element of utilizing social media effectively. Women in nonprofit leadership can share personal stories highlighting their organization's impact on individuals and communities. This approach humanizes their work and makes it relatable and inspiring for others. By showcasing testimonials, successes, and challenges, leaders can create a narrative that resonates with their audience, encouraging them to become advocates for the cause. Utilizing visuals like photos and videos can enhance this storytelling, making it more engaging and shareable.

Collaboration with other organizations and influencers on social media can also amplify the reach of a nonprofit's message. Women leaders can partner with like-minded organizations or influential figures with similar goals. This collaboration can take many forms, including joint campaigns, social media takeovers, or cross-promotional efforts. By tapping into each other's networks, they can broaden their audience and increase visibility for their initiatives, ultimately driving greater community engagement and support.

Finally, women leaders must analyze and adapt their social media strategies based on performance metrics. Understanding which types of content resonate most with their audience will enable them to refine their approach continually. Utilizing analytics tools available on most platforms can provide insights into engagement rates, audience demographics, and overall reach. By regularly assessing this data, women in nonprofit leadership can make informed decisions that enhance their digital presence and further their organizational goals, ensuring that their efforts yield meaningful community impact.

Engaging the Public and Media Relations

Engaging the public and fostering strong media relations is critical for women in nonprofit leadership, especially in education and community development. These leaders must leverage their storytelling abilities to connect with diverse audiences, including community members, stakeholders, and potential donors. Effective engagement begins with understanding the unique narratives that define their organizations and the communities they serve. By articulating these stories, women leaders can illustrate the impact of their work, inspire action, and build lasting relationships essential for sustainable growth.

To effectively engage the public, women leaders must utilize various communication platforms, including social media, newsletters, and community events. Each platform offers unique opportunities to reach different demographics and foster interaction. Social media, for instance, allows for real-time communication and feedback, enabling leaders to gauge public sentiment and adjust their strategies accordingly. Additionally, hosting community events can create a space for dialogue, allowing leaders to showcase their initiatives while listening to community members' needs and concerns. This two-way communication is vital for building trust and credibility.

Media relations are pivotal in amplifying women's voices in nonprofit leadership. Establishing strong connections with journalists and media outlets can result in broader coverage of their initiatives and successes. Press releases, media kits, and personalized pitches can help secure the attention of reporters interested in stories highlighting community impact and educational advancements. By cultivating these relationships, leaders can ensure that their organizations are portrayed accurately and positively in the public eye, ultimately enhancing their reputation and reach.

In addition to traditional media, the rise of digital platforms has transformed how nonprofits engage with the public. Women leaders must adapt their strategies to include blogs, podcasts, and webinars, which provide opportunities for deeper engagement and thought leadership. These formats allow leaders to share their expertise, discuss pressing issues in education and community development, and highlight the accomplishments of their organizations. Positioning themselves as thought leaders within these spaces can attract new supporters and collaborators who share their vision.

Lastly, measuring the effectiveness of public engagement and media relations is essential for continuous improvement. Women leaders should implement metrics to evaluate their outreach efforts, such as tracking social media engagement, analyzing website traffic, and assessing media coverage. This data helps in understanding which strategies are working and informs future initiatives and messaging. By remaining adaptable and responsive to feedback, women in nonprofit leadership can enhance their public engagement efforts, ensuring that they effectively empower communities and drive meaningful change.

Chapter 8: Measuring Impact and Success

Defining Metrics for Success

Defining metrics for success is critical in assessing the impact of women-led initiatives within nonprofits and educational institutions. Success metrics provide benchmarks that allow leaders to evaluate progress, identify improvement areas, and articulate their programs' value to stakeholders. In the context of women in nonprofit leadership, these metrics should be quantitative and qualitative, capturing the multifaceted nature of community engagement and transformation. By establishing clear metrics, organizations can better align their strategic goals with measurable outcomes, ensuring that their efforts are impactful and sustainable.

Quantitative metrics often include data on program participation, funding levels, and demographic reach. For instance, tracking the number of women a specific initiative serves can reveal the program's reach and effectiveness. Additionally, financial metrics, such as the amount of funding raised or the cost per participant, provide insights into the economic sustainability of programs. These numbers can be critical for securing future funding and support, as they demonstrate the organization's ability to manage resources effectively while delivering tangible benefits to the community.

Qualitative metrics, however, delve into the personal stories and experiences of those impacted by nonprofit initiatives. Surveys, interviews, and focus groups can yield valuable insights into how programs have changed lives and fostered community engagement. For example, assessing participants' feelings of empowerment or community belonging can highlight women-led initiatives' more profound social impacts. These qualitative measures are essential for capturing the nuances of success that numbers alone cannot convey, emphasizing the transformative power of leadership in community development.

Integrating quantitative and qualitative metrics allows organizations to picture their impact comprehensively. By utilizing a mixed-methods approach, leaders can report on statistical achievements and share compelling narratives that illustrate the human side of their work. This dual approach strengthens the case for support among donors and stakeholders and fosters a culture of reflection and learning within the organization. Leaders can use these insights to adapt and refine their programs, ensuring they remain relevant and responsive to their communities.

Ultimately, defining metrics for success is about establishing accountability and fostering a culture of continuous improvement. For women in nonprofit leadership, this means setting ambitious goals and being transparent about the challenges and successes experienced along the way. By articulating success and how it will be measured, leaders can inspire their teams, engage their communities, and secure the necessary support to drive meaningful change. As the nonprofit landscape evolves, so must the definitions of success, ensuring they remain aligned with the mission of empowering communities and creating lasting impact.

Tools for Evaluation and Assessment

In nonprofit leadership, particularly among women leading community-focused initiatives, the tools for evaluation and assessment play a pivotal role in measuring impact and success. These tools provide a framework for understanding program effectiveness and help articulate the value of nonprofit work to stakeholders. In the context of educational leadership and community development, selecting evaluation tools that resonate with the unique goals and challenges women leaders face becomes crucial. Utilizing Logic Models and Theory of Change frameworks can guide organizations in mapping out their objectives and the pathways to achieve them, ensuring that every initiative is aligned with broader community needs.

Qualitative and quantitative assessment methods should be employed to gather comprehensive insights into program performance. Surveys and interviews allow for the collection of rich, personal stories that highlight the lived experiences of beneficiaries, while quantitative metrics provide complex data on outcomes. Balancing these approaches for women in nonprofit leadership can enhance the ability to communicate impact to diverse audiences, from funders to community members. Engaging in mixed-methods evaluations can strengthen the narrative surrounding a program, illustrating both the statistical success and the human stories behind the numbers.

Technology has transformed the landscape of evaluation and assessment, offering innovative tools that streamline data collection and analysis. Platforms like SurveyMonkey or Google Forms facilitate participant feedback, while data visualization tools such as Tableau can present findings in an accessible and visually engaging manner. For women leaders in nonprofits, leveraging these technological advancements simplifies the evaluation process and empowers them to make data-driven decisions swiftly. Incorporating technology into assessment strategies can enhance transparency and foster a culture of accountability within organizations.

Moreover, peer evaluations and collaborative assessments can provide valuable perspectives that enrich the evaluation process. Partnering with other nonprofits or educational institutions allows for shared learning experiences and enables women leaders to refine their programs based on collective insights. By participating in community-based evaluations. Leaders can also strengthen partnerships and build trust among stakeholders, which is essential for sustained impact. This collaborative approach encourages a culture of continuous improvement, where feedback is actively sought and incorporated into future initiatives.

Finally, the importance of communicating evaluation findings cannot be overstated. Women leaders must be adept at translating data into compelling narratives that resonate with various audiences. Crafting reports highlighting key achievements and lessons learned while acknowledging areas for growth fosters a sense of transparency and engagement. By showcasing the impact of their work through effective communication strategies, women in nonprofit leadership can advocate for their programs, mobilize resources, and inspire others to join their mission of creating positive change within communities.

Communicating Results to Stakeholders

Communicating results to stakeholders is critical to effective leadership in the nonprofit sector, especially for women in leadership roles. The ability to articulate the impact of programs and initiatives builds trust and fosters a sense of shared mission among stakeholders. In educational leadership and community development, these communications can take various forms, including reports, presentations, and informal updates. Effective communication should be tailored to the audience, ensuring the message resonates with their interests and motivations. By emphasizing outcomes, leaders can demonstrate accountability and the value of their work, encouraging ongoing support and engagement.

One of the first steps in communicating results is to clearly define the metrics that will be used to measure success. For nonprofit women leaders, identifying relevant indicators helps track progress and demonstrates a commitment to transparency. This could include quantitative data such as enrollment numbers, graduation rates, community engagement statistics, and qualitative data like testimonials and case studies. By presenting a balanced view that includes both types of data, leaders can provide a comprehensive picture of their organization's impact, making it easier for stakeholders to understand and appreciate the value of their contributions.

In addition to the data, storytelling plays a vital role in engaging stakeholders. Narratives that highlight individual success stories or transformative community changes can evoke emotional responses and foster a deeper connection to the mission. Women leaders are often adept at using storytelling to illustrate the real-life implications of their work, making the results more relatable and compelling. By sharing personal experiences or testimonials from beneficiaries, leaders can humanize the data, illustrating what was achieved and the lives that were changed due to their efforts.

Furthermore, the format of communication should be strategic and diverse. Utilizing a mix of written reports, visual presentations, and interactive discussions can cater to different stakeholder preferences and increase engagement. For instance, infographics can summarize complex data efficiently, while community meetings allow for direct dialogue and feedback. In higher education contexts, leveraging digital platforms for webinars or online reports can broaden the reach and encourage participation from a wider audience. This multifaceted approach ensures that the results are communicated effectively and fosters a culture of collaboration and continuous improvement.

Finally, it is essential for women leaders to not only share successes but also address challenges and areas for growth. Acknowledging obstacles demonstrates honesty and can strengthen credibility with stakeholders. By framing challenges as opportunities for learning and development, leaders can inspire confidence in their ability to navigate complexities. Regularly updating stakeholders on both achievements and setbacks fosters an environment of trust and encourages collaborative problem-solving. Effective communication of results is not merely about reporting numbers; it is about building relationships, inspiring action, and empowering communities to thrive.

9: Inspiring Change Through Advocacy

The Role of Advocacy in Nonprofit Work

Advocacy plays a crucial role in the nonprofit sector, serving as a powerful tool for effecting change and advancing social justice. For women in nonprofit leadership, advocacy is a professional duty and a personal mission that aligns with their values and experiences. Women leaders can harness advocacy to address systemic issues affecting their communities by leveraging their unique perspectives. This approach amplifies their voices and empowers others to join in the pursuit of equity and justice.

Advocacy in nonprofit work involves raising awareness about specific issues, mobilizing communities, and influencing policymakers. Women leaders often utilize their networks to build coalitions focusing on pressing community needs. This collaborative approach enhances the effectiveness of advocacy efforts, as diverse perspectives contribute to a more comprehensive understanding of the challenges at hand. By engaging different stakeholders, women in nonprofit leadership can create a platform for dialogue and collective action, reinforcing that advocacy is most effective when it is inclusive.

Furthermore, advocacy is essential in shaping public policy and resource allocation. Nonprofits often operate in environments influenced by governmental decisions, making it imperative for leaders to engage with legislators and public officials. Under their lived experiences and insights, women leaders are positioned to articulate marginalized groups' needs. Their advocacy efforts can lead to developing policies prioritizing equitable access to resources, services, and opportunities. This direct engagement benefits the communities they serve and elevates the voices of women and other underrepresented populations in policy discussions.

In addition to influencing policy, advocacy serves as a means of capacity building within nonprofit organizations. By training staff and volunteers in advocacy skills, women leaders can foster a culture of empowerment and engagement. This capacity-building approach encourages team members to advocate for their causes, transforming them into active participants in the organization's mission. As they develop these skills, individuals become more confident in their ability to effect change, creating a ripple effect that strengthens the overall impact of the nonprofit.

Ultimately, the role of advocacy in nonprofit work is multifaceted, serving as a catalyst for change, a tool for empowerment, and a means of fostering collaboration. Women in nonprofit leadership are uniquely equipped to leverage advocacy to drive social change, drawing on their experiences and insights to inspire others. By prioritizing advocacy in their leadership approach, they contribute to the advancement of their organizations and play a vital role in shaping the future of their communities. This commitment to advocacy ensures that the voices of those often marginalized are heard and that meaningful progress is made toward social equity and justice.

Building Coalitions for Social Change

Building coalitions for social change is a vital strategy for women leaders in nonprofit organizations, particularly in public relations and higher education. Collaborative efforts amplify the voices of marginalized communities, creating a collective impact that individual organizations often struggle to achieve alone. By leveraging shared resources, knowledge, and networks, coalitions can address complex social issues more effectively. Women leaders, who usually bring unique perspectives and experiences, are well-positioned to foster these alliances, ensuring that diverse viewpoints are considered in decision-making.

Effective coalition-building begins with identifying common goals and values among potential partners. Women leaders must engage with various stakeholders, including community members, other nonprofits, academic institutions, and government agencies, to establish a foundation of trust and mutual respect. This process requires active listening and a commitment to understanding the needs and aspirations of all parties involved. By doing so, coalitions can create a shared vision that aligns with the interests of each member, enabling them to work together more harmoniously toward social change.

Communication plays a crucial role in maintaining coalition dynamics. Women in leadership should prioritize transparent and inclusive dialogue, ensuring that all voices are heard and valued. Various communication platforms, from social media to community forums, can help disseminate information and gather feedback, enhancing engagement. Moreover, fostering an environment where members feel comfortable expressing their opinions can lead to innovative solutions and strengthen the coalition's resolve to pursue its objectives.

In addition to effective communication, women leaders must navigate the challenges within coalitions. Conflicts may emerge due to differences in priorities, resource allocation, or decision-making processes. Leaders need to approach these challenges with empathy and a problem-solving mindset. Women leaders can help maintain the coalition's focus on its overarching goals by facilitating open discussions and negotiating compromises. This resilience strengthens the alliance and inspires confidence among members, encouraging continued collaboration.

Building coalitions for social change ultimately empowers women leaders to create a lasting impact in their communities. By harnessing the collective strength of diverse organizations and individuals, these coalitions can advocate for systemic change, influence policy, and drive social justice initiatives. Women's collaborative efforts in nonprofit leadership enhance their organizations and contribute to a more significant movement toward equity and empowerment. Through strategic coalition-building, women can transform their communities, ensuring that the voices of those most affected by social issues are amplified and heard.

Case Studies of Successful Advocacy Efforts

Case studies of successful advocacy efforts provide valuable insights into the strategies and outcomes of women-led initiatives in the nonprofit sector. One notable example is the campaign led by a group of women in education reform, which aimed to improve access to quality education for underprivileged children in urban areas. These advocates utilized data-driven approaches to highlight educational disparities, successfully mobilizing community support and attracting significant funding from local businesses and philanthropists. Their efforts culminated in establishing a community-based tutoring program, demonstrating how focused advocacy can improve educational outcomes.

Another compelling case study involves women leaders in environmental advocacy who sought to address the impact of climate change on vulnerable communities. By forming coalitions with local environmental organizations, these women conducted extensive research to document the unique challenges faced by their communities. They organized town hall meetings to raise awareness and engage residents, ultimately influencing local government policies to prioritize sustainable practices. This initiative empowered the women involved and fostered a sense of ownership among community members, illustrating the power of collaborative advocacy in driving systemic change.

In health education, women from diverse backgrounds campaigned to improve maternal and child health services in rural areas. They identified gaps in healthcare access and worked tirelessly to advocate for policy changes at both the local and state levels. Their efforts included grassroots organizing, storytelling, and leveraging social media to amplify their message. By partnering with healthcare providers and policymakers, they secured funding for mobile health clinics, significantly increasing access to essential services for mothers and children in their communities.

The success of these advocacy efforts is often rooted in the ability of women leaders to build networks and forge partnerships. A case study from a nonprofit focused on economic empowerment highlights how women entrepreneurs collaborated to advocate for policy changes that support small businesses. By sharing resources, mentoring one another, and presenting a united front, they effectively lobbied for legislation that improved access to capital and resources for women-owned businesses. This initiative demonstrated the strength of collective advocacy and showcased how empowered women can drive economic change in their communities.

Finally, the impact of these advocacy efforts extends beyond immediate outcomes, as they often inspire future generations of women leaders. Programs that emphasize mentorship and leadership development, such as those seen in the case studies, serve to cultivate a new wave of advocates who are equipped to tackle social issues. By sharing their stories and successes, these women create a legacy of empowerment and resilience, encouraging others to take up the mantle of advocacy. The ripple effect of their efforts underscores the importance of women's leadership in transforming nonprofits and communities, ultimately leading to a more equitable society.

Chapter 10: The Future of Women in Nonprofit Leadership

Emerging Trends and Opportunities

Emerging trends in nonprofit leadership increasingly highlight the importance of diversity and inclusion as fundamental components of effective organizational strategy. Women leaders in nonprofits are paving the way for innovative practices that enhance community engagement and foster a culture of belonging. Research indicates that organizations with diverse leadership teams are more likely to achieve superior performance outcomes. This trend underscores the necessity for public relations and higher education institutions to cultivate environments that prioritize diverse voices, particularly those of women, in leadership roles. Emphasizing inclusivity enriches decision-making processes and strengthens community ties, ultimately leading to more impactful nonprofit initiatives.

The rise of technology has transformed the landscape of nonprofit work, creating new opportunities for women leaders to engage with their communities. Digital tools and social media platforms allow for more direct communication and outreach, enabling organizations to amplify their messages and connect with constituents more effectively. Women in leadership positions are harnessing these technologies to create compelling narratives that resonate with diverse audiences. By leveraging data analytics and digital marketing strategies, they can better understand community needs and tailor their programs accordingly. This technological shift presents a unique opportunity for women leaders to innovate and drive change within their organizations and communities.

Another significant trend is the increasing focus on social entrepreneurship within the nonprofit sector. Women leaders are at the forefront of this movement, utilizing entrepreneurial approaches to address social issues and create sustainable solutions. This trend empowers women to take charge of their initiatives and encourages collaboration across sectors, fostering partnerships that enhance resource sharing and impact. Educational institutions can play a pivotal role in supporting this trend by offering programs that equip women with the skills necessary for social entrepreneurship, including financial literacy, strategic planning, and impact measurement. By nurturing this entrepreneurial spirit, organizations can build resilient communities capable of adapting to changing circumstances.

The importance of mental health and well-being is gaining recognition as a critical aspect of community development, particularly in the wake of global challenges that have tested the social fabric. Women leaders in nonprofits advocate for mental health awareness and support services, integrating these elements into their programs to promote overall community wellness. This trend reflects a holistic understanding of community needs and underscores the role of women leaders in fostering environments where mental health is prioritized. Higher education institutions can contribute by incorporating mental health advocacy into their curricula and training future leaders to recognize and respond to these vital community concerns.

Finally, the emphasis on sustainability and environmental stewardship is shaping the future of nonprofit work. Women leaders increasingly integrate sustainability practices into their organizational missions, recognizing the interconnectedness of social, economic, and environmental factors. This trend opens avenues for collaboration between nonprofits and educational institutions to address climate change and promote sustainable development goals. By engaging in interdisciplinary approaches, organizations can leverage the expertise of both sectors to create innovative solutions that benefit communities and serve as models for other organizations. This commitment to sustainability enhances community resilience and positions women leaders as pivotal figures in the fight against environmental challenges.

Preparing for the Next Generation of Leaders

Preparing for the next generation of leaders involves a multifaceted approach, prioritizing education, mentorship, and community engagement. As women increasingly take on leadership roles within nonprofits, creating an environment that nurtures their growth and prepares them for the challenges of tomorrow is essential. This preparation starts with recognizing women's unique challenges in leadership positions, including systemic barriers and the need for supportive networks. By addressing these issues head-on, organizations can lay a solid foundation for the future of women leaders in the nonprofit sector.

Educational institutions play a critical role in shaping the next generation of leaders. By integrating leadership programs focusing specifically on women and diversity, higher education can provide aspiring female leaders with the skills and knowledge necessary to navigate complex organizational landscapes. Curriculum development should include topics such as strategic planning, financial management, and advocacy, all tailored to address women's specific needs and experiences in the nonprofit sector. This educational framework empowers future leaders with the tools to effect meaningful change within their communities.

Mentorship is another key component in preparing women for leadership roles. Establishing formal mentorship programs within nonprofits can help bridge the gap between experienced leaders and emerging talent. These programs provide guidance and support and foster a culture of collaboration and shared learning. Organizations can facilitate knowledge transfer and inspire confidence in the next generation by connecting seasoned professionals with young leaders. Mentorship encourages women to take risks, voice their ideas, and aspire to leadership roles, creating a more inclusive leadership landscape.

Community engagement is vital in preparing future leaders, as it allows them to understand the needs and dynamics of the communities they will serve. By involving women in community-based projects and initiatives, nonprofits can provide real-world experience invaluable for leadership development. Engaging with diverse populations helps emerging leaders develop empathy, cultural competence, and a deeper understanding of social issues. This experiential learning enriches their leadership skills and fosters a commitment to community empowerment and social justice.

Finally, organizations must prioritize the creation of an inclusive culture that values diversity in leadership. By actively promoting women to leadership positions and advocating for equitable practices, nonprofits can model the change they wish to see in society. This includes reevaluating hiring practices, offering professional development opportunities, and creating policies that support work-life balance. When women see themselves represented in leadership roles, they are more likely to envision their potential as leaders. This collective effort to prepare the next generation of leaders will ultimately lead to stronger, more resilient nonprofits capable of driving meaningful change in their communities.

Creating a Legacy of Purpose and Impact

Creating a legacy of purpose and impact in nonprofit leadership requires a deep commitment to cultivating individual and community growth. Women in these leadership roles often bring unique perspectives and experiences that can significantly shape the mission and vision of their organizations. This influence is particularly crucial in the nonprofit sector, where the focus is on fostering community development and driving social change. By aligning personal values with organizational goals, women leaders can create a lasting legacy that resonates through their communities.

One of the cornerstones of building a legacy is the establishment of clear, actionable goals that reflect the community's needs and the organization's aspirations. Women leaders have the opportunity to engage in collaborative processes that include diverse voices from the communities they serve. This participatory approach empowers community members and ensures that initiatives are relevant and sustainable. By prioritizing inclusivity, women leaders can foster environments where stakeholders feel valued and invested in the outcomes, enhancing the overall impact of their work.

Mentorship plays a pivotal role in creating a legacy of purpose and impact. Women in nonprofit leadership should actively seek to mentor emerging leaders, particularly young women who aspire to follow in their footsteps. By sharing experiences, providing guidance, and facilitating networking opportunities, established leaders can help cultivate the next generation of changemakers. This investment in future leaders strengthens the nonprofit sector and helps perpetuate a culture of empowerment and resilience within communities.

Furthermore, integrating innovative practices and adaptability is essential for sustaining a legacy. The nonprofit landscape continuously evolves, influenced by changing social dynamics, technological advancements, and funding landscapes. Women leaders must remain vigilant and responsive to these changes, utilizing them as opportunities for growth and transformation. By fostering a culture of innovation within their organizations, they can create impactful programs that address pressing community needs and set a benchmark for effective leadership.

Ultimately, creating a legacy of purpose and impact involves a commitment to lifelong learning and reflection. Women leaders should regularly assess their contributions and the effectiveness of their initiatives, seeking feedback from stakeholders and community members. This reflective practice enhances personal growth and informs future strategies, ensuring that the legacy they leave behind is one of genuine transformation and enduring value. Women can inspire others to join the movement toward more equitable and thriving communities by leading purposefully.

www.ingramcontent.com/pod-product-compliance
Lightning Source LLC
Chambersburg PA
CBHW081101180526
45171CB00003B/400